# Nina Campbell
# INTERIORS

# Nina Campbell
# INTERIORS

PHOTOGRAPHY BY Simon Brown

CICO BOOKS
LONDON  NEW YORK

*For Rita, Max & Alice*

Published in 2013 by CICO Books
An imprint of Ryland Peters & Small Ltd
519 Broadway, 5th floor, New York, NY 10012
20–21 Jockey's Fields, London WC1R 4BW

www.rylandpeters.com

10 9 8 7 6 5 4 3 2 1

Text, design and photography
© CICO Books 2013

A CIP catalogue record for this book is available from the Library of Congress and the British Library.

ISBN 978 1 78249 054 8

Printed in China

Text: Meredith Etherington-Smith
Copy editor: Alison Wormleighton
Designer: Christine Wood, with Alison Fenton
Photographer: Simon Brown
(photographs on pages 202–235 John Butlin)

PAGE 2 A comfortable bar in the corner of the billiard room in China (see pages 202–235). Note the bottles of Chinese firewater on the top shelf – drink these at your peril!

PAGE 3 Paisley half-shades add a twist to the more conventional wall lights in the guest loo of the Swiss chalet (see pages 130–161).

THIS PAGE A silver-plated tray with a stylish set of 1930s champagne coupes. With a striking painting by Anselm Kiefer and the clock in its glass box, this makes a beautiful black and white tableau (see pages 68–87).

# contents

# introduction

My life as an interior designer began at an early age. My parents moved house frequently, though mostly around Belgravia, and I was always allowed to choose what my own room looked like. In fact, I made some rather sophisticated attempts at decoration.

In my career I have been lucky enough to travel all over the world, working in different countries, with widely varying customs. One of the most extraordinary journeys involved breakfast in Shanghai after leaving the house you will see in this book, which was three hours by car from Shanghai, and finished with dinner in Jordan, where I was working on a house in Amman. It was the most extreme cultural change in a twelve-hour journey I can imagine.

I think my approach to any new job is the same whatever and wherever it is: basically I am there to be a guide to achieving the clients' desires and to be the editor of their dreams. I believe that the most successful homes come from an enjoyable journey made together to achieve the end result. At the beginning it is important to find out how extensive the work will be. As you will see, some of the houses in this book have had major surgery while others have just been given a facelift. I must admit I do find it exciting to build a house from scratch, as was the case with the house in China, but equally I love restoring an old house to its former glory, as with the 19th-century relic of more glamorous times in New York.

The budget is obviously a vital thing to discuss from the first. I have found that it is always possible to add to it later, but very difficult to cut it down partway through. Being honest about how you really want to live in the house is also an important piece of information. Do the dogs live on the bed, for instance? Is the kitchen going to be the centre of family life or will it be used more for catering large parties? Do you want to lie full length on the sofas and read, or sit tucked up in an armchair? Accurately answering all these and many more questions helps to achieve a home that is right for you.

OPPOSITE This pierced screen overlooks one of the two internal gardens in the centre of the Chinese house (see pages 202–235).

Speaking as an inveterate shopper, I think interior design is the perfect job, because it is one's duty to be looking around constantly for new things, whether they are antique or contemporary pieces, and major pieces of furniture or accessories. I don't just look in antique shops and markets – wherever I am, I also visit art galleries and exhibitions. And, of course, magazines and shops are often good sources of new inspiration. Even if these ideas are not relevant to my current projects, they will be stored away in a corner of the brain, to resurface later when appropriate. I find that almost any shopping expedition can end up with a good idea, even when I haven't actually purchased anything.

There are certain things that are really important to any successful interior, though, strangely, they are not necessarily the things you notice. I feel it is really important for a house to run in a calm and orderly fashion, and in order to achieve this you need as much well-organised storage and as large a laundry room as possible. There is also that magic place, the housemaids' cupboard, which is absolutely vital, with or without a housemaid!

Once this is all sorted out, the fun can begin. I try to use anything that a client brings to the house, as old favourites are important. Sometimes they need a bit of a makeover, but that can be very rewarding.

For me, however, what makes a perfect interior is that it is never totally complete. A house should be finished to the point that it is comfortable, is somewhere that you can live and entertain, and looks finished, but it must always have a few spaces yet to be filled. If nothing ever changes, a house can become stagnant.

Today, for example, I had an amazing morning with my New York client, who is in London for a couple of days. We found a wonderful early Caucasian rug for the landing from Gallery Yacou. On a roll, we then went to visit Adrian Sassoon in search of one or two objects to put on top of a pair of 19th-century columns in the study. It is impossible to go to Adrian's without finding something, and we bought an incredibly beautiful pot made by Walter Keeler, to go with an equally mouth-watering piece by the ceramicist Kate Malone. My collector client also rang to say that a Picasso drawing had just been delivered, and he wanted me to go over to the apartment to find a suitable place for it. All this adds to the excitement of this career.

The houses and apartments in this book are some of my latest commissions. They range from a house so big it is a virtual palace in the middle of China, to a tiny pied-à-terre, a collector's apartment and a country house in London, as well as taking in a contemporary chalet in Switzerland and a very grand 19th-century house in New York. Each of these homes involved very different requirements and problems, and the clients were equally diverse. I hope you enjoy looking at the solutions I have come up with as much as I did decorating these places and making them homes to enjoy living in.

OPPOSITE A collection of Staffordshire cottages from the client's collection sit amongst the books in the family room of the London country house (see pages 88–121). A view of the marble fireplace through the gilt mirror in the drawing room of the same house.

# memories of 19th-century new york

My client came to me having seen my work at The Brook, a men's club in New York which, being a brownstone, was a similar type of building to his house. It was an exciting commission and it just goes to show that good things happen to those who wait, because this is a building where my client originally lived while at university, in a third-floor flat. He shared the flat with various people and then entrusted it to a friend, but with the proviso that they had to move out the minute he wanted it back. This occurred two years later, by which time he was able to buy the flat, and then slowly, slowly, he bought the rest of the building.

About five years ago my client was finally able to do what he'd always dreamt of doing, which was to restore the whole building and turn it into a private house. I doubt that it had ever actually been a house previously, because, rather like New Town houses in Edinburgh, it would probably have been built as an apartment block. The clue to this was that the staircase was not central, as it would have been if this had ever been a house, but went up the side of the building.

My client asked me whether I could recommend an architect and I thought of Kevin Lichten, with whom I'd worked at The Brook and who would be ideal because he's a restoration architect. Work started, during which the back of the house virtually fell down. This caused serious delays to the programme as the entire back had to be taken down to the foundations and rebuilt. New permissions were needed, and city departments in any country work at their own pace.

OPPOSITE The new staircase, from the top of the house looking down.
The mottled dark green runner links the whole house.

OPPOSITE My client did say to me once, 'Do you think it would be completely mad to have an elephant in the hall?' Because I love elephants and was brought up on Babar the Elephant books, I said, 'No, of course not. I think it would be magical,' and I set about thinking how on earth was I going to find an elephant. I was in India, staying in Delhi with a friend, Momin Latif, and I said to him, 'I know this is a really stupid question but do you know where I could find an almost life-size baby elephant? I'd like an ebony one.' And he said, 'Well, you obviously didn't look very carefully when you came into the drawing room – look outside.' And in his hallway was El the elephant. I negotiated with Momin and bought it immediately. He is seated on a beaten bronze plate, but he also needed a plinth which I had made of hardwood stained black. Finally, we bought the elephant an incredibly beautiful antique rug to stand on.

ABOVE The mahogany-panelled landing was designed to house this beautiful landscape by Jane Wilson. The stool is a lucky purchase from a Sotheby's sale, fitting the space perfectly and also offering some protection to the painting. The picture light above was custom made by Collier Webb.

OPPOSITE Looking through to the red lacquer library/dining room from the landing, through the brilliantly scaled arch, a feature common to the landings throughout the house. It provides a great frame for the view of the dining table and central window.

OVERLEAF Inspired by the first years of the 19th century, this dining room is as near as I'll ever get to introducing Sir John Soane to Edith Wharton.

OPPOSITE AND BELOW More views of the red lacquer library/dining room. The candelabra are hugely over-scaled, which looks very dramatic against the red lacquer. This is a dining room entirely designed to be used at night and is lit by a mixture of electric and candle light. The bookcases are washed with light from the Besselink and Jones swan-arm lights, and there are four hurricane shaded wall lights with burgundy candles, like the one seen below. The mirrored slips set into the bookcases are a nod to Sir John Soane. The dramatic painting above the fireplace is 'Red Rocks and Sea' by Roderic O'Conor, brilliantly spotted in a sale by my client.

OPPOSITE AND BELOW Detail is everything, from the red bead trim on the blackberry taffeta blinds, to the silver car cruet which I turned into flower transportation. The table is set with silver underplates and silver animal cruets, this elephant being one of them. In sharp contrast to the red lacquer are the dining room chairs covered in an acid green and blackcurrant check by Claremont Fabrics.

The house dates from the 1860s. I love the slightly unimposing, pinkish-toned brownstone facade with its relatively small front door on the ground floor. This leads into a lobby (see pages 12–13), off which are cloakrooms and huge closets, providing space for hundreds of coats. My client is a party-giver so these are essential. There is also a basement devoted to storage and a fully equipped catering kitchen. El the elephant guards what we loosely term the Ritz-Carlton, which is the guest suite – a sitting room, bedroom and bathroom leading on to a double garden because my client also owns the building next door.

From the lobby you sweep up the new stairway (see page 11) designed by Kevin Lichten in the centre of the house; it is really beautiful, like a Brancusi sculpture. What Kevin has done with the architecture is lovely. On every landing, for instance, wide arches create great vistas to the rooms beyond, which, like the staircase, are new. A green runner is laid on the stairs all the way to the top floor, but it is interrupted by the landings, because these are almost rooms in themselves, especially on the two floors used for entertaining. On one of these landings I put bookcases and a place where a bar can go when a big party is being held.

Because the staircase curls up a shaped wall, which you cannot hang pictures on, I chose a wallpaper that would give some interest without being so dominant that it would compete with the contents of the house. This is a man's house and it is filling up rapidly with things because he's an avid collector. In addition, I wanted the wallpaper to reflect the period of the house while also having a contemporary feel, so it could go right up to the top floor. I therefore chose the large-scale but muted damask-patterned Veneziano paper from my own collection.

The beautiful staircase leads you up to the floor where the dining room and kitchen are sited, and which has dark wood floors throughout. On the same floor is a lovely big kitchen. On one side there is a simple table with Windsor chairs and a door going down to the garden, and on the other side is the working kitchen. On the walls is a collection of photographs of chefs – one pointing at you, and others peeping out of windows – bought in Venice, and there's a television. It's a comfortable, everyday, working kitchen.

OPPOSITE Revealed across the landing through an arch is the kitchen, divided into eating and working areas. This leads down, via a terrace, into the private garden.

BELOW LEFT, BELOW RIGHT AND OPPOSITE The gents' loo, where William IV in the shape of the restored washstand meets photographs of the Jazz Kings. The wallpaper, Amati, is a rich red with a Moorish design in a deeper red and gold which brightens this small room. I hope guests can find the basin when the top is down!

The dining room is quite English in feel and definitely 19th century in inspiration (see pages 15–21). It is actually a library/dining room, with bookcases built around the walls. Here I was influenced by Sir John Soane's idea of having mirrored slips between bookcases.

The bookcases and walls are lacquered red and the blinds are a beautiful blackberry taffeta. I commissioned the carpet from Parsua – with its soft green background and the reds in the pattern, it adds a lightness to the room. Above the fireplace, which was made for us by Jamb, is a wonderful painting, *Red Rocks and Sea*, by the Irish painter Roderic O'Conor.

The dining chairs started out as a set of six 19th-century English chairs that my client had purchased, and then I copied them for another 12 chairs so that 18 people can be seated around the table. There are also three window seats. The whole room can be candlelit, so it's very glamorous at night, especially as the mirrors make everything sparkle. Above all the bookcases are lights washing the books with ambient light. I added lanterns on all four corners of the big ceiling, and a chandelier over the table, so that there would be a lot of different lighting opportunities.

Also on this floor is a guest loo, for which I found a William IV washstand (see pages 24–25). It came from Alexander von Westenholz, where I had gone looking for something completely different, as one does. When I asked what it was, he told me it was an old washstand, so we opened it and, of course, it was completely decrepit inside. I bought it immediately and brought it here. We lined the inside of the top with mirror, put a proper marble base in it and plumbed it for the States. The wallpaper in this room, called Amati, is from my wallpaper range and is overprinted in gold, which adds light and glamour to an otherwise dark little room. And there are more wonderful photographs on the walls here.

OPPOSITE AND OVERLEAF Up one floor from the library/dining room, to the first view of the drawing room cum music room. To make this room light and tranquil, I used a palette of silvery greys punctuated with amethyst and acid green. The walls are covered in a totally plain dove grey wallpaper called Canto, from my collection.

PREVIOUS PAGES LEFT The four-seater sofa is covered in grey chenille. Above it hangs my client's collection of J.B. Yeats drawings and an oil painting, including the central self portrait and two drawings of Yeats's great friend, the celebrated poet and renowned beauty Jeanne Robert Foster. Adding fun are the leopard-skin and crimson damask cushions.

PREVIOUS PAGES RIGHT One of a pair of oval carved 18th-century mirrors painted in soft green and water gilt. The two crystal and nickel arm lights are placed low on the chimney breast to add a little sparkle to this corner and not shine in the eyes of people on the seats.

OPPOSITE Leopard-skin and crimson damask are an amusing combination. The buttoned Isabella chair has green velvet surrounding my Delamont cut velvet with its coloured stripes. The 18th-century black and gilt chair is easy to pull up; I covered it in the same Delamont fabric. The leopard-skin Daisy chair can also be moved to join one of the seating groups.

OPPOSITE The convenient bar is tucked off the landing. I wallpapered it in my black and gold Stradivari wallpaper. The woodwork is painted black, with the well of the ceiling and the door architrave in a dull gold mottled paint. The bronze sink and the thick glass shelves make this an enticing space to mix a cocktail.

BELOW On this landing a log trolley goes up and down in the lift. It was a piece of engineering, which involved Kevin Lichten and myself working on the problem of getting logs that are stored in a sub-basement up to each floor for the log fires lit every day. Our solution was this reinforced-steel trolley that wheels in and out of the lift. I love overcoming complications to make life easier – it's what design is all about. The cupboards were built so that the trolley could slide in. It's kept on the drawing-room floor because that is where the main fires are. On the way up, it can be stopped en route, to dish out wood wherever required.

You climb the stairs to the next floor, unless of course you take the lift, and come to a drawing room that spans the whole front of the house. The room is really a music room. A grand piano occupies a central position in the room – my client is an accomplished pianist and has very musical friends, so the room is furnished in such a way that a lot of people can sit down to listen to music or talk. On either side of the fireplace, there are Lehmann benches covered in a rich amethyst velvet with a pair of leopard velvet-covered Daisy chairs to one side and to the other, two Isabella chairs in an acid green and deep red stripe. On the wall opposite is a comfortable four-seater sofa and chairs to expand the seating area for guests. Twelve of us were there recently and we occupied only half of the room.

This room was designed to be subtle, with a soft grey wallpaper and curtains providing an elegant but muted background. The rug is a bronze/green silk and wool cut pile, Rio Rita, designed by me for Stark. On the pale grey wall above the sofa is an interesting collection of drawings and an oil by J.B. Yeats. At the moment there is a tantalisingly empty space above the fireplace, waiting for the right painting. I believe that decorating a house is an ongoing journey, and it is wonderful to still have spaces to fill.

At the back end of this floor is a cosy sitting room cum study. The mix here is really interesting, from a serious set of six maps to a rubber elephant and a bronze bullmastiff staring at a tortoise. It is all about having the things you love around you. There's comfortable seating upholstered in a Bennison fabric, and the wallpaper is my Canto Stripe in a soft green and gold. At the back of the room is a big corner sofa overlooking my client's own terrace, which we built for him at treetop level. It looks all the way down an incredible secret garden with massively high trees, so it's like being in a huge tree house. He doesn't have access to the garden, which means he doesn't have the responsibility of looking after it but has all the pleasure of looking at it.

OPPOSITE Across the landing from the drawing room, another arch leads into the sitting room cum study.

OVERLEAF In the sitting room cum study, the plain Parsua rug with the dark green border has already withstood a lot of wine. The front and back of this room are quite eclectic. On the left the chairs are covered in a Bennison linen print which I also used for the curtains. The chair in the foreground is upholstered in Robert Kime's striped velvet.

PREVIOUS PAGES I designed the comfortable green chesterfield, covered here in my dark green Bovary chenille. The wallpaper is the green and gold Canto Stripe which I often use. The fireplace can be seen through a handsome convex mirror with its original glass. The bear above the sofa is a Navajo rug; this room houses quite a ménage of different animals.

BELOW The decorative picture of a boy with a monkey on his shoulder tops the specially made fireplace, guarded by two rhinoceroses.

OPPOSITE I often employ details such as beading, gimp and fringing when finishing the upholstery on chairs. I am particularly pleased with the strié horsehair on the club fender.

OPPOSITE The back of the study is dominated by sectioned corner seating which overlooks the terrace. My Amisi chenille is used for this seating. The carpet is an antique rug which brings together the whole eclectic feel of the room. The painting above the sofa is 'Two Friends' by Wright Barker.

BELOW This lovely printed velvet from Robert Kime is on the seat of a 19th-century English cane bergère, found at HRW Antiques. The cushions are in a wool carriage cloth, with cords and edgings to pick up the colours of the room.

OVERLEAF French windows allow the back part of the study to flow out on to a new terrace which overlooks a secret garden. We furnished the terrace with outdoor furniture from McKinnon and Harris.

The house has such generous space that there is room for his-and-her master suites. In her master suite, which was very loosely inspired by both Marie Antoinette and the 1930s, everything is pretty and French, with a spriggy blue-and-white wallpaper, a feminine bed and a little sofa at the end of the bed with a painted coffee table. The bedroom leads into a beautiful Carrara marble bathroom, where the Roman blind fabric looks almost as though it had been hand-painted. Also adding to the feminine look are a 1930s Bagues chandelier, a 1930s steel and marble dressing table and a little bathroom chair.

I very much enjoyed creating this pretty and feminine bedroom suite. The owner of this room is a writer and wanted a space to be able to write in a tranquil surrounding. The layout of the floor allowed for a very spacious dressing room off the bedroom, with packing tables, so the bedroom needs no clothes storage. For me, this is the height of luxury. The walls are papered in blue sprig Folco paper, which I think has a French flavour, the curtains are white cotton damask, trimmed in blue, and the headboard is covered in a silver grey satin. Although rarely shut, there are sliding doors leading to a white marble bathroom. This room is flooded with light, and the walls are a beautiful blue that matches the blinds at the windows. On one side of the bed is an Italian painted chest of drawers, and on the other a round table with a pale blue taffeta cover, housing a lamp and photographs.

I think a sofa at the end of the bed makes a room very inviting; this one faces the fireplace. There are bookcases to each side of this classic white marble fireplace, and also the desk, so this space really did fulfil all that was asked of it.

OPPOSITE The inspiration behind her master bedroom was a charming French bandbox. I used my Folco wallpaper, which is a small-scale trellis with a floral motif, in blue and white. The little end-of-bed Audrey sofa is upholstered in a pale blue and grey Delamont.

BELOW AND OPPOSITE Above the classic white marble fireplace from Jamb is an antique Venetian mirror. The 1930s Bagues chandelier with glass drops and beads adds glamour to the bedroom. A corner of the Audrey sofa, upholstered in Delamont, with a cream paisley silk cushion trimmed with cream silk-covered beads. The dressing table stool is covered in a soft blue fabric from Claremont, piped in white. A detail of the 1930s dressing table in the bathroom.

PREVIOUS PAGES This bathroom, like all the rooms in the back extension of the house, looks all the way down the gardens and, as a result, the rooms have wonderful light and privacy. The bathroom has a very large and comfortable bath under the window, with the vanity unit facing it. Georg Lauth, who works with me, is a particular wizard at creating glamorous bathrooms and this is no exception. The 1930s chrome dressing table, complete with its own mirror, fitted perfectly into the rather small space. Above is a small watercolour by Jane Wilson. The long view of the bathroom shows the blind in my Silvana cotton, which features delicate, seemingly hand-painted flowers. This was inspired by a wonderful sketch book of botanical drawings that I found.

OPPOSITE AND BELOW The vanity, with mirrored cupboards for extra storage above, has two beaded appliqué wall lights, set on to the mirror. These are from Niermann Weeks and add to the feeling of the Gatsby years.

My client wanted something calm at the top of the house, therefore his master bedroom leads into a sitting area where he can watch television, if he ever does. This is very much a private domain: there are lots of family photographs, and the back part of the room is a particularly comfortable area where he can read and think. Every room needs to have an armchair with good light for reading.

His dressing room is a cosy room where he can relax in front of an open fire. I had the fireplace made in mahogany and in front of it there's a sofa covered in one of my fabrics. We found a stool when we went up to Connecticut shopping – believe it or not, it had just been sent out from England the week before. We had some cupboards made from oak in William IV style.

I had to slightly persuade my client with regard to some details, such as trimming the edges of the walls with a flat green braid so that the room would look more finished. The blinds, made from a masculine tweed, are bound in green velvet, to echo the braid trim on the walls without matching too obviously. The rug is by Parsua. Nearly all the rugs I used in this house are contemporary, though a few, such as the one underneath the elephant in the lobby (see pages 12–13), are antique rugs from Robin Yacoubian of the Gallery Yacou.

OPPOSITE On the landing at the top of the house, double doors lead into my client's dressing room.

OVERLEAF The mahogany bolection-moulding fireplace, which was specially made, has amusing sketches hung above it and is home to a collection of pigs. The textured-check blinds are made of my Crosslee Weave bound in sage green velvet, and the stool is covered in the same fabric. The comfortable chesterfield is covered in my pure wool Broughton Weave.

ABOVE One of the many animals living in the house! A bronze elephant standing on a book, in front of a dark red leather-covered lamp from Collier Webb.

OPPOSITE We discovered this early 19th-century bow-fronted chest of drawers on a shopping trip to Connecticut. It had been made for a gentleman's dressing room and so is very much at home here. I think all rooms are improved by a piece of good furniture. The mirror reflects the cupboards on the other side of the room — they are all custom made, albeit to resemble a wardrobe.

Beyond my client's bedroom is a handsome and comfortable marble bathroom with a massive shower at one end and a huge bath at the other (see pages 66-67). The room is a link between the bedroom and the dressing room, and is also swiftly turning into a photographic gallery. The walls are painted a mole brown, which is a great background for the black-and-white photographs. There is a trio of photos of an old man and a child sitting chatting in deckchairs on the beach. On closer inspection you see Charlie Chaplin, and the little girl is the daughter of the painter of the beautiful green landscape on the landing (see page 14) – I do love these circles in life.

I feel that in this house, designed for an interesting and thoughtful client, past meets present to create a very special atmosphere.

OPPOSITE The master bedroom and the dressing room are linked by the bathroom. The bedroom has the same linen on the walls as the dressing room. I corded it in a sage green to pick up on the colour in the Bennison print on the armchair and the headboard.

OVERLEAF Details of the bedroom with the fireplace and the armchair for reading in front of the fire. In the window there is a stool with an antique Middle Eastern woven document. And, of course, there are more pigs on the mantelpiece.

OPPOSITE AND BELOW Because it is an internal room, the bathroom has a large skylight, which floods it with light. The bathroom is of grey and white Carrara marble with a taupe wall and a gallery of family photographs. The bathroom wall lights are from Carlton Davidson and date from the 1950s.

# peace and light for a collector

This is an apartment I decorated for a Russian couple who have come to live in London. He is a major collector of really important contemporary art – some of it frankly quite challenging – which needed to be fitted into the decor without being overwhelmed by it. My clients are both passionate about music, concerts, football and good food and wine. In other words, they are very cultivated people, and they enjoy living in a calm and pleasant way. Because they travel a great deal, they need to relax when they arrive in London.

I can only describe the apartment as a 1970s leftover. However, it had terrific potential space as it was on the first floor of a grand Victorian building in Belgravia. Three French windows gave on to a drawing room with high ceilings and a balcony. The bedroom had the same handsome proportions and there was a good dining room and a kitchen. But when we found it, all the doorways had been narrowed, the ceiling had been lowered in the hallway and the plasterwork had been painted a putty colour. My clients' brief to me was very simple: 'light'. They were desperate for more light so we opened up the whole apartment. She was adamant that she didn't want any colour at all, just neutrals, although I did manage to introduce some muted shades of bronze. This was rather fun for me, as I had never done an interior entirely in neutrals before. Instead of colour, I went for texture. And when I realised they were going to bring in some serious art, this neutral background made a great deal of sense to me, because suddenly the neutrals not only provided the right background for their art collection but were also very light-reflective and restful.

OPPOSITE The newly widened doorway into the drawing room reveals a spectacular antique chandelier I found for my clients. You can also see the specially designed carpet with a 1930s scroll border which echoes the curved legs of the central table.

OVERLEAF The Giacometti chair is counterpointed by the new neoclassical marble fireplace. The sofa by Christian Liaigre is covered in a slubbed silk chenille.

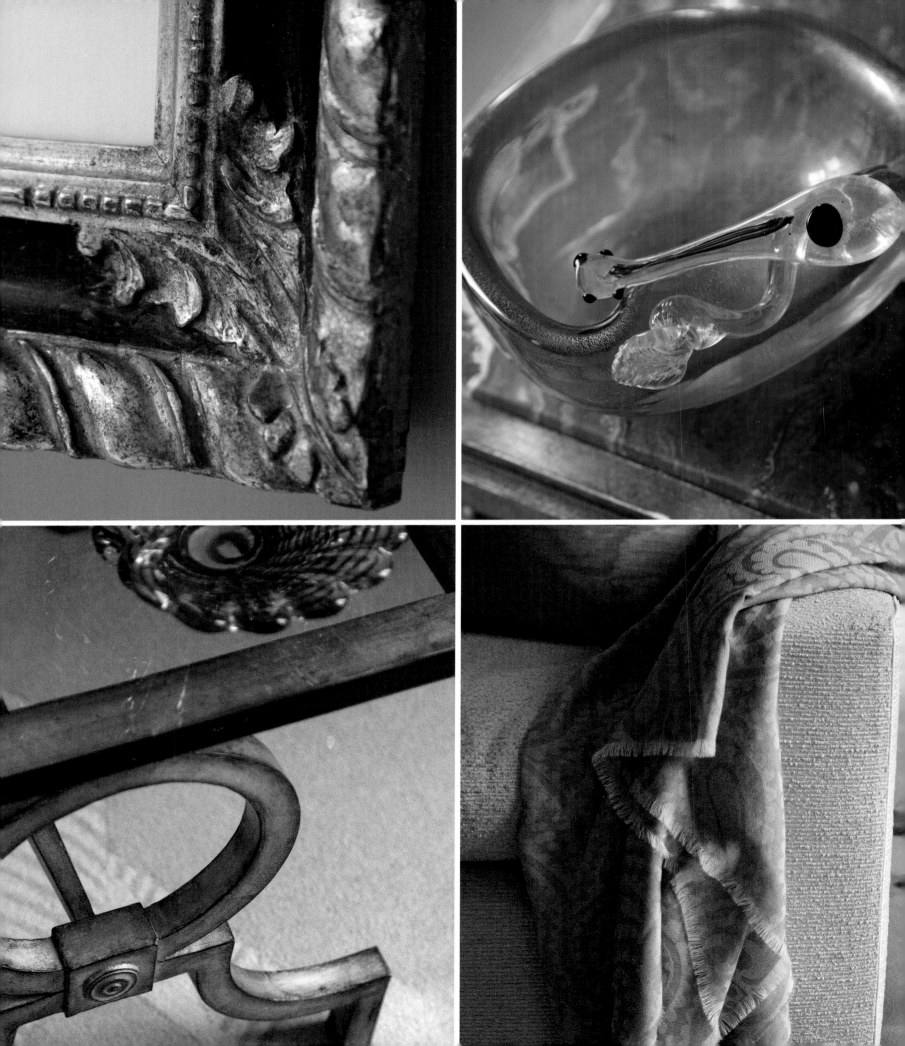

OPPOSITE The details in this apartment all have a strong 1930s flavour and include a 1930s Murano ashtray with a musical feel, an elaborate frame for a contemporary painting and strong glass and brass side tables inspired by 1930s design.

BELOW A view over the alabaster table to the tulip painting by Kuper. The Botero ballerina glides across the table.

First, however, I had to eliminate the work of the 1970s developer, opening up the whole apartment to create more light and better spaces. The bathroom, for instance, had been cut in half, with one side becoming the bathroom for the guest room, and the other side a horrible bathroom off the main bedroom.

At the end of the bedroom, there was a narrow room which we opened up to a certain extent, but we wanted to leave a small, somewhat private room in which my client could have his desk and bookcases. You now go through this to the bedroom, so it's like an anteroom.

It was important to introduce a laundry room for washing and storage, to carve out a decent second bedroom and shower room, to create a very good main bathroom with a shower, separate toilet, bidet, bath and everything else, and to create a walk-through dressing room.

I will admit we vacillated about the spare room – it's almost always the husband who doesn't want anyone to come to stay. Now there's a very large exercise ball and a massage table in this exquisite spare room, but it is nevertheless very comfortable should anyone come to stay.

The most important new detail in the drawing room was the marble fireplace, which goes with the 19th-century architecture of the building. I felt the fireplace had to be appropriate for the ceiling, the plasterwork cornices and the French windows, but after that we could do what we felt like. My client wanted a piano so I bought him a Steinway for the drawing room, and I think when they settle into their new home they will ask young musicians to come and play.

To decorate this newly revealed space, I combined the neutrals and varied textures with contemporary furniture to achieve a 1930s feel. In the drawing room are quite modern sofas from Christian Liaigre. We had rugs specially made for the drawing room and the dining room; based on 1930s designs, they were woven in a trompe l'oeil effect in France. The rug in the dining room has tone-on-tone musical instruments in the border, and the drawing-room rug is in the same style, but the border was designed using inspiration from the Braquenié archive.

OPPOSITE For the dining room I bought dining chairs in 1930s mode and a really wonderful vase for the dining table because in such a calm atmosphere you only want one or two good flower arrangements. Quite often in the drawing room my client uses just a few flowers such as white tulips, which won't fight with the art.

LEFT The Botero sculpture stands on a stone plinth and guides you into the dining room. The rug, which was specially designed with a border of musical instruments, complements a similar rug in the drawing room. Everywhere you look in this collector's apartment great art is beautifully displayed – here, for instance, you can see the Giacometti wall light to perfection. The dining table was designed by Lucien Rollin. The curtain fabric is from Watts.

The drawing room curtains (shown on page 69) are made from a textured Ravelli fabric with a horizontal stripe. The poles are of almost invisible Perspex which nudge up to the rather over-elaborate cornice, so here we've created a dialogue between grand Victorian, 1930s and contemporary.

There's a large table with a handsome orange alabaster top and we bought a chandelier with big rock-crystal drops. The whole room was conceived as a marriage between then and now, and the chandelier does not overpower the owner's splendid boot by Georg Baselitz. The Giacometti chairs also look good against this deliberately understated background.

The clients brought only their art and a few small pieces of furniture and objects to their new apartment, so we bought a 1930s bronze patinated coffee table. They also brought funny little tables from their previous flat which work nicely. Actually, I rather like it when people bring some things of their own, because they have a patina and inject their own personality.

To continue the 1930s theme in the bedroom, I had bedside chests made in shagreen, and there's a wall of cupboards with handles you can hardly see. The walls are covered in a white linen, the throws are our lovely paisleys and the bed linens are all embroidered by the Monogrammed Linen Shop to complement the room. We commissioned a glass table and added some little chairs that are modern copies of Louis XV designs from the André Arbus collection, one of his typical 1930s designs with historic shapes.

The clients loved the finished apartment. It works because it is all now a relatively empty and peaceful space. Wooden floors go all the way through, linking the rooms, and the colours – or rather, non-colours – go all the way through too. The shades of 'white' alter very faintly through the apartment, so the whole place forms a background for whatever my client buys for his art collection, which will change constantly. He's still buying and collecting so we go into despair mode when something else arrives because there really isn't anywhere to put it. Eventually something will have to go to maintain the feeling of peace and light.

OPPOSITE Under a small part of the owner's art collection is a bronze Charles lamp – this is an original, made in the 1930s. The console is by Giacometti.

OPPOSITE AND BELOW This little office leads through into the master bedroom. I commissioned the bookcases because in such a small space it was impossible to fit in normal bookcases. There is a pair flanking the painting and they mirror the archway that goes through to the bedroom. The step sculpture by Yuri Kuper came from the collector's previous house.

OPPOSITE The bedroom has a dramatic Angelo Donghia chandelier. The walls are lined with linen. The serpentine 1930s-inspired chests covered in shagreen were commissioned by me from Garrison Rousseau. The bedhead, designed and made by us, is covered in ash-coloured satin, as is the chair.

OVERLEAF The curtains are an embroidered silk from Rubelli. I bought the striking 1930s console and grey mirror for the bedroom. I have no idea who made the table but it is fabulous and continues the 1930s theme. The mirror is by Fontana Arte from Robert Dickson and Lesley Rendall Antiques.

FOLLOWING SPREAD On the left, the walk-through dressing room with folding cupboard doors leads to the newly sited pale white and grey-veined marble bathroom. The mirrored double basin reinforces the 1930s look, as does the trolley, which is an original.

# a london country house

A charming lady who used to live in the north of England came to London to find both a country house and a London flat, but ended up with one very big, lovely house (almost a country house in fact), near enough to London to pop in whenever she likes. Having lived in her previous home for a long time, she had not changed anything for ages, so her new house was an adventure. My job was to go on the journey of decorating the new house with her and make sure she enjoyed the process, which I think she did – she says she's loved every moment of it.

My client, who had recently parted from her husband, has a grown-up family that is beginning to expand, and they do still come and visit at weekends. I think it's always difficult when there's been a split, because you keep some things from your old life but not others, and maybe you have only part of something like a dinner service, so you have to readjust. Luckily my client has an open mind and realised very early on that her new home was going to be completely different from her former house. It was going to have a much fresher approach which would be all hers. When my client first moved in, the drawing room – which is the least necessary room that anybody ever has – became a storeroom. This proved very useful, as we could go there and pick and choose, reassembling her things in new and different ways.

The first thing I decided was that it must be a family house and not be precious. On the stairs, for instance, I decided to buy mouse-coloured carpet, rather than coconut matting, which everyone slips on. So we got a stair carpet in a good old taupe shade ('back of mole' as John Fowler called it, and indeed 'taupe' is the French word for a mole) and it strangely brought the whole house together.

OPPOSITE View of the family room, which is off the kitchen and is the hub of the house on the lower ground floor. As you come down the stairs it looks welcoming and cosy, with bookcases full of china and books, a television, plus comfortable sofas and armchairs – a room to relax in with your nearest and dearest.

OVERLEAF Children's books and a collection of charming Staffordshire cottages are displayed on the bookshelves in the family room. The lovely Queen Anne desk is a good place to sit and write letters in the middle of the din!

OPPOSITE The armchair incorporates all the colours of the family room in my floral fabric called Montacute. The sofa is covered in a grey chenille, which relates to the soft grey of the walls, and the curtains are in an olive Bicton stripe. The whole room is done in muted shades of olive, red and grey.

BELOW Two cushions from the first Nina Campbell Cushion Collection pick up the colour theme of red and beige on pale grey linen.

OVERLEAF Creating magic in a room lies in a careful attention to detail as you can see in these photographs of the family room, whether it is the textured velvet chairs or the parquet floors. The David Linley games table was specially made for the room and has all the names of the children carved around it. The chairs around the games table are covered in olive Gilty fabric with an olive suede cloth on the outside back.

When you first come through the front door into the hall, you go down three steps straight into a warm, cosy study which looks on to the garden. Being a keen gardener, my client can sit in here and admire her handiwork. Taking all her books into account, I decided to use French grey as a background colour and then line the bookcases with red, so that there would always be a cheerful colour coming through. We've put her red wing chair in this room, and she can work on the table near the books.

The lower ground floor, which came off the kitchen, did not work at all for my client, so I laid wooden floors and put down rugs. We blocked up two windows in the family room either side of the fireplace because they looked on to a brick wall of the house next door and gave no light. It takes quite a lot of courage to block off a window because one's instinct is to think in terms of increasing the light, not reducing it. But we blocked them up and put large built-in bookcases in their place. Now there's a perfect spot for the television, which is buried in the bookcase opposite a sofa facing the fireplace.

The bookcases also provide an ideal display area for my client's Staffordshire collection and her funny cottage tea sets, as well as plenty of storage space for the family's books – rows of Enid Blyton tales just waiting for the next generation – plus puzzles and board games. These are played on a wonderful table made by David Linley with all the family's names on it. A beautiful and rather grand Queen Anne desk has a prime site at the window, where my client can sit and write.

OPPOSITE The study can be shut off from the rest of the house and is a quiet room looking out to the wonderful garden. The client already owned the inlaid kneehole desk.

OPPOSITE On the floor of the study is a multicoloured strié carpet, which brings warmth and cosiness to the room. The wing chair belonged to the client and is upholstered with red corduroy velvet on the outside. The ribbing echoes the stripes of the carpet, while the colour picks up on the needlework patchwork on the inside. Everything in this room sprung from the chair.

BELOW I added the wraparound bookcases in the study, covering up an opening into the dining room. The bookcases are lined in red, repeating the colour of the chair and making them more fun – I love to line bookcases in another colour!

OVERLEAF The dining room was originally painted this colour – a lovely Swedish blue grey – and we added some colour to the equation with the embroidered floral curtains from Pierre Frey. My client already had the chest-on-chest, and it seemed a perfect place to store all the table linens.

The dining room also led off the study through a doorway which we blocked off. We took the steps out and created a cupboard in the dining room, which will be incredibly useful for china and glass. My client had left behind some very classic dining room furniture in her old house, and having six children, she is bound to end up with more than a dozen people for lunch in the not too distant future. I therefore designed a new formal dining room for her, but incorporating more contemporary furniture. A pale oak table and chairs make the area lighter, and there's also a chest-on-chest and a corner cabinet – it's always nice to have two good pieces in a room. Over the fireplace is a painting by Lucy Jane Cope, which she had commissioned for her previous home. The colour proved to be magic in the dining room, a perfect punch of joy.

We had originally hoped that the walls of the drawing room (see pages 108–114) could be left the colour they had been painted, but in the end the yellow shade proved dingy and light-draining. The existing fireplaces were very nice and in fact my client bought quite a few things from the previous owners, including the drawing room rug. It is predominantly made up of reds and blues, and the curtains in this room are now in a bold appliquéd linen in the bright and deep reds of the rug. In one corner of the room there is a built-in banquette, which is upholstered in a wide-striped velvet, and it faces the insanity of a pair of little leopard-skin bucket chairs. I love them because they're silly and fun and make the room less pompous. There's also a pretty settee-type sofa that three young children could certainly jam themselves in, with a pair of chairs upholstered in a red, cream and green fabric set either side, opposite the fireplace. And a comfortable red chair is tucked alongside the piano, so twelve people can now sit in this room in comfort.

OPPOSITE We made the long oak table and the dining room chairs. The client's painting by Lucy Jane Cope looked perfect above the fireplace and the set of ten botanical prints were also her own – there were just the right number to fill the rest of the panels.

Given the presence of the grand piano, and the fact that music is a big part of my client's life, it is likely that anyone gathered in this room will be enjoying some music. In fact, the room is more a music salon than a drawing room. It's interesting that there's a grand piano in all the drawing rooms I've designed in the last year or two, and in New York (see pages 28–29) there is a music room as well. If you've got the space, it's rather nice to have that – you don't just need another room with two sofas and two armchairs.

I've loved being able to incorporate the things my client had brought with her, such as the leopard-skin chairs, as well as wonderful finds like the early 19th-century Baltic chandelier, which just lifts the drawing room. I think it's incredibly important to have things from the past in a home, especially if there's been an upset in a family such as a divorce. When the children come into a room in a new house and they recognise things that they've known all their lives, albeit arranged differently, they start to feel attached to the house, and the owner has a feeling of belonging and also a breath of new life. We've kept the formal side of life at the front of the house, but when the young come to stay at weekends, their more informal needs can also be accommodated. Everyone can join in a musical evening in the drawing room, Sunday lunch can be laid out in the dining room, Saturday lunch can be comfortably taken in the kitchen, and there's also scope for a cosy telly supper in the family room.

Down some steps from the drawing room, was a very cold conservatory (shown on pages 115–117) – it was absolutely icy! It obviously was a room that nobody had cared about much. There was a door out of it leading to a spiral staircase down into the garden, and as this wasn't necessary we shut up that door and boarded up some side windows looking on to the

OPPOSITE This table is the end piece to the long dining table we made and is used as a side table when it is not needed to make up the length. The mirror is oval and 18th-century Irish carved wood, inset with some very old glass beads. The flower vases are a collection – I like it that they are tall enough that flowers are reflected in the mirror.

OVERLEAF The little silver salt and pepper figures are a reference to the client's Dutch forebears – a nice family touch. I think the octagonal three-tiered table looks just right against the window bay. The curtains are a Pierre Frey embroidered floral fabric.

neighbouring house. Now people can spill into the conservatory from the drawing room and sit on a corner banquette. At one side of the steps up to the drawing room is a little marble-topped painted bar, and on the other side is a corner unit with a cut-glass mirror. The windowsills are filled with cut flowers and things that my client has collected such as a chain sculpture and wooden birds. An important part of my job with this house was to create new arrangements from all the assorted items that my client had brought with her, whether they went together already or had never been juxtaposed previously.

We had some good luck on one of our shopping expeditions. Having set out thinking we probably wouldn't find anything, it turned out to be an exciting day. We found two girandoles, now in the conservatory, which just screamed 'Hello, I need to go on that wallpaper'. We placed them to look as if they were almost growing out of the paper (see page 115). On that same trip, we came across a ravishing Baltic chandelier, which is now in the drawing room, and an extraordinary Murano cranberry glass lamp which was totally unnecessary but so perfect that it had to be bought. It now sits next to the piano.

I had to do this house piecemeal while my client lived in it, which might have been difficult. But she has been thrilled by what has proved to be a happy journey, and I think she's now loving her new life and all its details. That was what made me passionate about decorating and arranging this house.

RIGHT The formal drawing room doubles as a music room, as all the family play an instrument. The carpet came with the house and the splendid Baltic chandelier was specifically bought.

PREVIOUS PAGES I maintained the red and beige theme set by the curtains and had the sofa made for the seating group opposite the fireplace in the drawing room. The art and the sculpture on the table already belonged to the client.

OPPOSITE The client's own inlaid table holds a collection of Murano cranberry glass and a treen box.

BELOW The corner seating in the drawing room is upholstered in brown, beige and red wide-striped velvet. With the little leopard-skin pull-up Daisy chairs, it makes a cosy grouping.

OPPOSITE The wallpaper in the conservatory is one of mine and has a Swedish feel. It looks like boarding, and you can buy both the plain boarding pattern and the boarding with flowers stencilled on it, so that you can create the effect of a painted room while varying the amount of stencilled flowers according to your own preferences.

BELOW We bought the drawing room's Baltic chandelier on the same trip as the sconces, one of which can be seen opposite. This detail of the chandelier shows just how intricate the waterfall effect is.

PREVIOUS PAGES The stone tiles in the conservatory were inherited from the previous owner. It didn't seem worth taking them up but they weren't cosy enough for a room adjoining the drawing room. We therefore created a rug out of some marvellous rubbery matting in an olive green shade. It has an affinity with the garden and brings the whole look together. Two wacky chandeliers resembling birdcages provide light at night, and there's another light on the table plus a couple of spots that can be lowered. The effect is quite saucy, with sexy lighting at night.

OPPOSITE Telling details include the client's architectural model, and her duck decoy. The fabric used on the corner banquette is Boxgrove and the fabric on the bergère is Elcho.

LEFT The rooster was a family favourite so I painted this little lobby between the kitchen and the utility rooms red to house him and to bring all the doorways together. It worked, because it cheered up a rather gloomy little space.

OPPOSITE Luckily the kitchen didn't need touching. It was white and very streamlined, and as my client is a great cook, that was an excellent place to start. I decorated the eating area with a stencilled-effect floral wallpaper. We built in a dresser in the kitchen which we painted a murky green to hold cookery books and china. A rustic table and Windsor chairs, with cushions covered in a painted rose fabric, give a farmhouse feel to one end of a quite slick kitchen. I also made a wall of windows that slides right back, so when the weather is warm enough, the whole eating area becomes almost outdoors. Outside, there's a big paved area with two tables. A bench is painted a wonderful deep greenish bronze shade.

# a fishy tale

This was my third time decorating the Capital Hotel's dining room, now called Outlaw's after Nathan Outlaw, the current chef, who specialises in seafood. I was delighted to be asked by Kate Levin, the daughter of owner David Levin, who runs the hotel, to redesign the restaurant and bring it up to date. The first time I decorated it was in the 1970s, after the Irish terrorist bombings which were going on in London at the time. The dining room had originally been built in the 1960s with huge plate glass windows, which were deemed dangerous, so we had to cover them up with heavy curtains. Now light is suddenly back on the menu and I was able to reveal the windows and, in fact, get rid of the curtains altogether.

I have to be honest and admit that this is an awkward room. Not only is it very tall and rather thin, but what I inherited on this particular journey was panelling at the ends and around the middle – there was a lot of yellowish wood that needed to be balanced. I decided to remove the panelling from the wall leading into the kitchen and paint it an incredible, luminous fish-scale turquoise. The chef has a fishtail as his logo, which was the inspiration behind this. By having this small section of the restaurant painted in such a shimmering colour, your eye goes beyond the panelling and creates a sense of perspective. Then we went back to a previous incarnation of this plain blue wall and reopened the window on to the kitchen, which had been open when I first did the dining room.

OPPOSITE I've used mirrors a lot in Outlaw's restaurant in London's Capital Hotel. Here, mirror is set into the panels between the windows, themselves revealed now that the curtains have been replaced by Roman blinds.

OVERLEAF One of the pair of newly lowered and cleaned chandeliers which form dazzling focal points of this mirrored and panelled room.

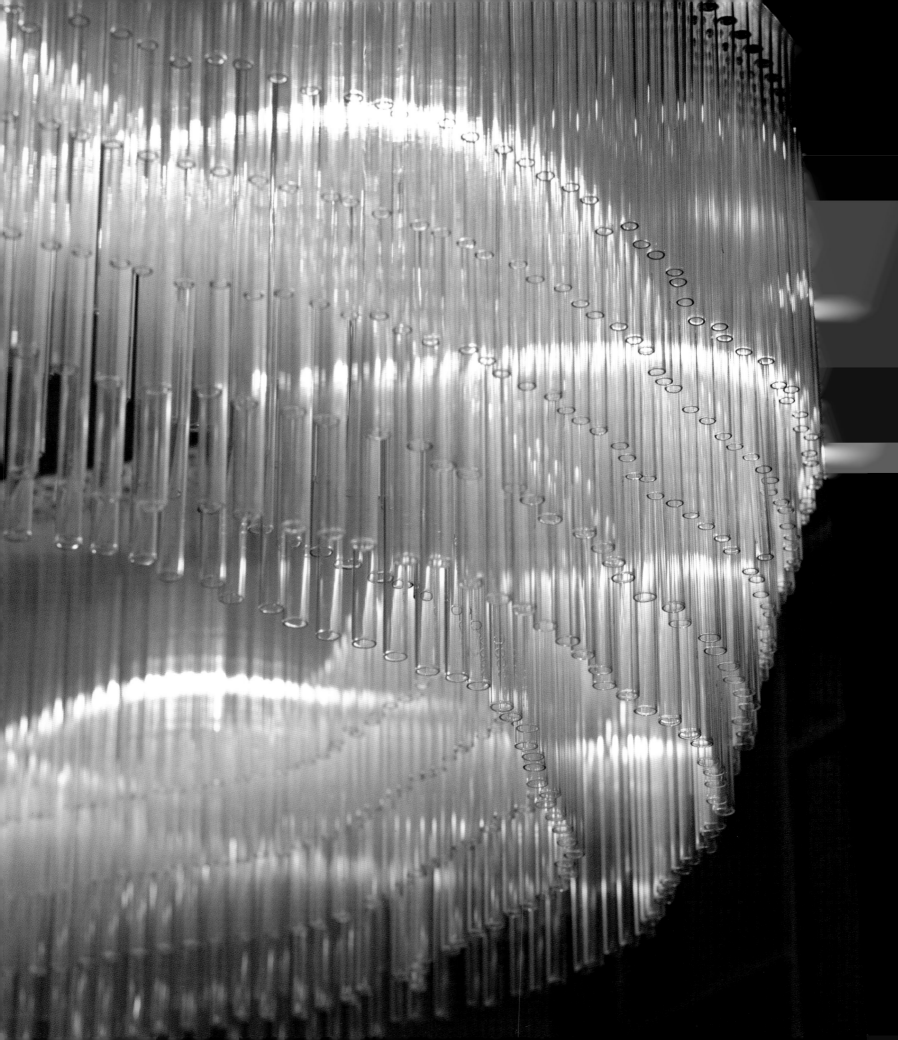

There are a lot of mirrors in the restaurant, reflecting light all around the room. The two chandeliers were already there and are rather wonderful, but when I first walked into the room I thought they looked a bit strangled. We cleaned them and lowered them considerably, so that now they not only reflect into the mirrors but also sparkle, now that there's no more smoking to dull their glitter.

For the Roman blinds, which are partly down most of the time, I used a bronze print on a teal ground, so the effect is rich but still contemporary and not overpowering. The chairs were there already, and as they are always an expensive item in a hotel, we just re-covered them. On the front we put a plain blue fabric and on the back we used a fabric that is woven to resemble basket weave, but that I think looks like fish bones. A little bit of fun!

We opted for plain wooden tables with dark tops laid with Chilewich mats, which look like brown linen. This was because the whole point of the restaurant this time around is that, although it serves incredibly delicious food and is one of London's top restaurants, eating here is meant to be a little more casual, a little more relaxed than it was in the past. It's a more contemporary approach.

To complete the room I found a pair of wonderful pictures of seahorses, again in metallics, and we put these at either end of the restaurant. The hotel also had some nice watercolours and prints, and I simply reframed them so they went together in a new way. The result, I like to think, is light, fresh and delicious – just like Nathan Outlaw's food.

OPPOSITE Between the original panels I hung a pair of seahorse prints with a metallic finish. Like the Hubbard flower prints on page 190, they come from Natural Curiosities, where they are silkscreened and silver-leafed.

OPPOSITE The chairs were the hotel's own, but I re-covered them in Boxgrove on the back and Fursdon on the front, both fabrics from my range. Nathan Outlaw, the chef, wanted to reveal the original opening we'd had between the kitchen and dining room, which had subsequently been covered up. This gave me the opportunity to remove the panelling and substitute the beautiful turquoise paint effect resembling lacquer, to brighten and lighten the room even further.

BELOW This antique trolley, from the collection of the owner of the Capital Hotel, David Levin, probably dates from around 1900.

# a chalet in the vernacular

This Swiss chalet in a setting of alpine fields is the second or third house I've done for Italian clients, who tend to have an appreciation of good design, enjoy buying well and want to be comfortable. Although the owners of this chalet entertain to a certain extent, they have two young children so the chalet is for the family and friends with children to ski in the winter and to relax in the summer. In Switzerland even the summers are not going to be boiling hot – there's no swimming-pool life outside – and the chalet is built of wood, inside and outside, so I made the rooms rich and darkish to counterbalance the wood.

It is rare for me to work in as vernacular a style as I have done here – it's all quite folkloric – but I think the Swiss style really works. What was good about this particular chalet was that it was built by a master craftsman who had huge warehouses of traditional wooden doors and ceilings and carved things, so it is Swiss through and through. In these circumstances, you have to just go with the flow. There is no point trying to do modern.

When you arrive at the chalet, there is likely to be snow on the ground. However, this house has an underground passage, so you can park under cover and then walk through the corridor and up in a lift to the front door. The entrance is quite small with a cupboard for all the snowy coats; nobody's going to arrive without a coat in winter so you might as well make sure there's somewhere to put them. For fun I included a traditional antler bench with striped wool upholstery which picks up all the colours I have used throughout the chalet. Red was always going to be very dominant in this house and I added a slate grey which reflects the colours of the winter sports posters my clients have collected.

OPPOSITE The chalet's magnificent surroundings, viewed through the front door. The wood and granite floor in the outer hall links the outside of the chalet to the inside.

OPPOSITE The entrance hall with the stone and wood floor that makes the transition from the stone outside to the wood floors in the rest of the house. The antler bench is covered in a multicoloured striped wool fabric that picks up the tones of the floor and the framed poster above it.

BELOW The very Swiss staircase has an extremely practical, tough carpet of reds, browns and beiges that brings all the colours of the house together. On the wall is one of the many historic Swiss travel posters the client has collected over the years.

WINTER SPORTS IN FRANCE

You go from the outer hall into the inner hall and up the staircase, with its traditional wooden banister. The striped carpet echoes the colours of the fabric on the antler bench and elsewhere.

I also decorated the lift because you'll be in it for a couple of minutes. I put fabric on the walls and added a poster and a nice light rather than a ghastly light bulb, so at least you have something to look at – I think lifts are the new things to decorate!

Leading off the landing is the open-plan living room, which is quite a large space (see pages 138–139). The fireplace faces you as you come up the stairs, so there's a sofa, a table behind it and chairs around it. On either side of the fireplace are two small windows, where I put window seats to give extra seating. So as not to have curtains in the window seats, we used mirrored shutters. These are fun because they reflect the marvellous scenery while they're open and then when they're shut they're covered in fabric.

ABOVE LEFT On the stairway walls, 'shield' wall lights are distinctively Swiss. You can imagine the Swiss guard holding them up to defend the Pope!

LEFT AND OPPOSITE The lift has fabric-covered walls and also features more vintage travel posters.

ABOVE AND OPPOSITE On the first-floor landing, we
decided to add a drinks tray as we had quite a bit
of space and it seemed a good use for it. The tray is
placed on a rather good piece of 'old' painted Swiss
furniture. The client is very particular about his bar –
he always has a good one and likes to find glasses
that are very special. I love these annual Swiss
glasses all painted with different years on them.
Antique glasses are great to collect even when they
don't match, and this sort of harlequinade of glass
makes a drinks tray look very inviting.

OPPOSITE The long view of the drawing room. To balance the walls, I added red wool curtains at the windows with wide paisley borders and we used an alternative paisley on the French chairs. For a bit of fun, I threw in the two little fireside slipper chairs in Pierre Frey's embroidery-effect Swiss Miss fabric, which takes us straight back to the Swiss vernacular. The large bronze and glass coffee table is packed with books and dishes holding delicious sweets.

OPPOSITE AND BELOW LEFT The dining area of the room is dominated by a yacht table made by Soane for the house to fit the space. It is mahogany with brass banding and brass supports. I added very comfortable nubuck-covered and nailed chairs.

RIGHT AND BELOW RIGHT The small windows either side of the fireplace are closed by shutters lined on the inside with red paisley. When the shutters are opened and folded back to the sides, they reveal mirror, reflecting the landscape outside. Underneath the windows are window seats, which form the perfect log store, just as it would have been in an old chalet.

The fabrics on the chairs in the drawing room include rich, warm paisleys by Etro. The curtains are red wool with wide borders of a red paisley on the bottom, bordered in plaited cord. The French chairs, which can be pulled up when needed, are upholstered in a whiter version of the paisley. The whole room is decorated in a palette of rich blue-greys, reds and off-whites. It is comfortable and unfussy, with practical touches such as the logs stored neatly under the window seats. The cushions are beautiful Italian cut velvet, which I added just to throw in something different.

Round the corner is the TV area which has a sort of modified plaid carpet that echoes the front hall in reds and greens. Here, I massed tartans and paisleys together, as I think they make a wonderful mix. There's a large wrap-around sofa covered in red, a comfortable big armchair and bookcases.

My favourite objects in this room are a ravishing red Art Deco Cartier clock and a leather coffee table made out of luggage. There's a great sense of place – of being in Switzerland – right the way through the chalet, so how could I resist a snow globe on the table? We've all had one and sneered at it, but it's such fun.

At the other end of the room (there's a kitchen on that floor) there's a rather marvellous long ship's table which came from Soane, and we had chairs upholstered in bashed-up nubuck leather and then nailed (see pages 140–141). They are easy and comfortable and eight to ten people can sit round that table.

LEFT An enormous television is set into a handmade wooden bookcase. The blinds are made from a dark green carriage cloth, bound in red. Beneath them is a supremely comfortable corner sofa covered in my scarlet Bovary chenille. The carpet brings all the colours together.

OPPOSITE AND BELOW Red paisleys are used for the cushions and a deep border on the curtains in the drawing room, while a paisley with a light background strikes an echo on the French chairs. The red enamel clock is a 1930s piece by Cartier and the snowstorm globes add the finishing vernacular touch.

OVERLEAF The spectacular view from the wraparound balcony outside the sitting room, with McKinnon and Harris loungers covered in white Sunbrella fabric piped in coffee.

The master bedroom is upstairs. My clients didn't want a very feminine bedroom so I did the bed in chocolate-brown velvet lined in a cosy cream wool and then trimmed the edges with braid. One thing in the bedroom is rather practical: my clients wanted be able to lie in bed and watch a movie – don't we all? So I had made a very slim chest in the same Swiss style for the foot of the bed. The TV pops up from it, clad in wood, and disappears when it isn't being watched. After all, when you're in Switzerland and you've come back from skiing, it's snowing and you've just had a hot bath, you would want to watch television.

OPPOSITE AND BELOW Looking through the four-poster bed across the bedroom with its high wooden ceiling and linen damask on the walls. The bed is hung with brown velvet curtains lined in cream wool and tied back with blue and brown rope. The braid edging the curtains is in the same colours as the rope.

ABOVE LEFT AND OPPOSITE Striped Roman blinds, in Fandango Stripes and bordered with caramel Troubadour, make a play in the bathroom where a bronze steel tub commands the middle of the room. I placed the tub next to the window so you can lie in the bath and look out on to the fields.

BELOW LEFT As you go through the door into the master bedroom, there is a wonderful lobby and a walk-in dressing room. The builder had some antique painted doors in his warehouse and I felt it would be rather fun to have them in this house, as a door to the walk-in wardrobe.

We used a predominantly red and white scheme for this spare bedroom, which has a lot of wood in it. The curtains and the bed came from the guest room in a previous house I did for these clients, as the arrival of another child meant that that guest room had to be turned into a nursery.

The curtains are in the red and white Petit Gonesse fabric by Pierre Frey. I used a sweet little trellis pattern print in red and white called Lussac from Braquenié on the walls and edged it with red cord. It picks up the trellis pattern of the cane headboard. The bed is flanked by bedside tables with card-shaded lamps on them and is covered in a delightful throw featuring an appliquéd reindeer – the perfect present from a clever guest.

As you lie in bed, you can gaze up at the panelled ceiling stencilled in a traditional patterned effect – being Switzerland, details such as this are incredibly well done. On the wall opposite the bed is my clients' collection of gently comic winter sports cartoons. A pretty, spriggy fabric is used for a comfortable chair by the French doors on to the wraparound terrace.

OPPOSITE A charming red and white fabric from Pierre Frey curtains this small guest bedroom, perfectly framing the stunning view from the wraparound balcony where tables and chairs make it the perfect spot for drinks on a summer's day.

OPPOSITE Plump and comfortable down-filled cushions in the Petit Gonesse fabric and the red-and-white seaweed pattern make a comfortable place to have a well-earned nap after skiing.

BELOW I used a woven cotton fabric called Lussac from Pierre Frey on the walls of the smaller guest bedroom, bordered with a fat red cord, knotted in the corners; fabric surfaces help to make wooden rooms quieter.

OVERLEAF The larger guest bedroom has a bold wool fabric called Pomegranate on the walls to make this high-ceilinged room cosy. The two single beds have carved headboards, padded in dark green linen to match the curtains and bed skirt. Also made in Switzerland are the small bedside tables with lined wicker baskets.

The ceiling is very high in both the master bedroom and the larger guest bedroom, shown on the previous pages. On the walls here I used a fabric of mine called Pomegranate in a wonderful wool. I think that staying in this room would be magical because you'd feel very cosy and warm and enveloped in comfort. I did very high headboards, with two beds that interlink; a dark green valance, bordered on the bottom, echoes the green coarse linen of the curtains, which have a very chunky looped border. I had little bedside tables made and had baskets lined in another small-scale fabric.

The top floor is the children's floor (seen overleaf). In their shared bedroom they have two bunks built in like a train, and little chairs. It's a great big lovely room where they can play, and there's a funny little walk-in playhouse with charming Pierre Frey European Ski fabric. There are also little window seats where they can curl up and read books; it's all typically Swiss.

Knowing these clients well, what I think works so well is that this chalet couldn't be anyone else's — it's completely personal. Very much a family holiday place, it's incredibly comfortable and they absolutely love it. What is so wonderful about sitting in the warm, richly coloured rooms here is the distant sound of the bells ringing on the cows as they chomp away at the buttercups in the fields outside.

OPPOSITE Cheerful details from the larger guest room — a detail of the cut velvet cushion, the over-scaled braid on the edge of the green linen curtains, the dimity-printed linen from Nicole Fabre used to line the bedside baskets and a detail of the headboard against the Pomegranate fabric.

OPPOSITE AND BELOW His-and-hers Pullman bunks in the children's eyrie
at the top of the house. I chose fun, playful Swiss nursery fabrics for the
curtains and cushion covers, and all the miniature furniture was made
by the builder/architect. The bathtub, which we painted a nautical red,
white and blue, has a porthole in it.

# a london pied-à-terre in miniature

My clients for this miniature pied-à-terre are a neat, meticulous couple who live in America now. He is English by origin and she is American. They bought this small-scale flat in London as a little nest because they travel a lot and use their London base as a springboard to travel in Europe. It's a typical top-floor flat in a mansion block that looks out over the tops of trees and a large communal garden, so it has plenty of light. And it still has all its original 1930s architectural details, such as metal-framed Crittall windows and streamlined mouldings.

My client had trained as an engineer so he had great fun planning everything. When it came to the kitchen, he worked with me to make sure we could get the air conditioning in – he found the smallest possible air-conditioning unit, which was a good thing as the flat really is tiny and the kitchen is no more than a galley. Thanks to his planning, we got more in it than most people could in a kitchen twice the size – it was like doing an extraordinary jigsaw puzzle.

The flat was dismal when we started. It had dreary colours, wall-to-wall carpet and that generally musty atmosphere of a 1950s service flat, and my clients wanted to give it back its 1930s feel. Before we altered the flat, you would come through the front door into the usual long corridor, which I always think is so depressing. It had a door leading into the living room and then went on endlessly with doors off it – something I really can't bear. I opened the flat up by putting in etched-glass screens made by my friend Guillaume Saalburg in Paris. Now you come through the front door into a hall, which feels like a proper room because of the glass screens. The etching on the screens prevents you from immediately seeing the living room, while the opening between the screens creates a sort of reveal. Similarly, when you're in the living room or dining room you don't feel as though you are sitting in the hall.

OPPOSITE I designed two small bronze console tables to go in the hall on either side of the screen for keys, post and suchlike.

PREVIOUS PAGES This mirrored wall was created for me by Guillaume Saalburg to double the drawing room in visual size. Two sofas by Lucien Rollin are covered in Fortuny fabric and are copies of 1930s designs, to go with the client's own furniture. The walls of the drawing room are covered in pale blue satin, and the same fabric was used on the curtains, with a shaded gimp on the leading edges. The whole point was to make this small room feel light, airy and much bigger.

OPPOSITE AND BELOW Details are all in Art Deco mode – a set of Carlo Moretti glasses on the drinks tray, a detail from a table lamp, a cranberry glass match striker, the deco-inspired gimp from the edge of the curtains and a vase of flowers that sits on a 1930s dining table.

As you go past the screens, the dining room becomes visible on the left-hand side, and in the dining room there are sliding doors leading to the kitchen. When the couple are entertaining, these doors can be slid back to reveal a kitchen that I made to look more like a sexy bar, in dark marble. It's actually filled with equipment like washing machines, and the air conditioning is buried in there somewhere so you don't see it. There's a stable door from the kitchen on to the balcony, which we also redid as it wasn't very nice.

The wood we chose for the dining room floor is used in the living room too (and throughout the flat, to make the space feel larger). The mirrored wall at the end of the living room, opposite the windows looking over the gardens and treetops, was also done by Guillaume and increases the space and light. With the wooden floors (and no rugs) in mind, I chose pale blue satin for the walls. We had this paper-backed and stuck on the walls and used the same fabric for the curtains. As a result, the whole room is all about space and reflection. The sofas, which I bought from Tatiana Tafur, are good 1930s copies. We covered them in a Fortuny fabric, again in the same light, airy style, and we found a pair of 1930s-inspired bucket chairs which we covered in red velvet. All the furniture had to be comfortable, but small in scale to match the size of the flat.

OPPOSITE For the dining room, I found a beautiful 1930s dining table. My client, who enjoyed buying a lot of the furniture, then went shopping in Paris and found a sideboard and a painting to go over it; he also found the chairs. The result is a proper late 1930s dining room glamorous enough for Tamara Lempicka herself.

PREVIOUS PAGES In the master bedroom, the walls are lined in beige linen finished off with cord. The curtains are in a horizontal silk in the same shades.

OPPOSITE The master-bedroom cupboards, meticulously planned to answer every storage problem, were painted in a cross-hatch paint effect to blend with the linen on the walls. The small two-tone cord is used around the room as a finishing touch.

BELOW The bedside tables in the master bedroom were specially made with a drawer and fixed to the wall in order to maximise this tiny space. The lights were mounted on the wall for the same reason.

OPPOSITE AND RIGHT In such a tiny space detailing really is important but must be kept light and simple. Shine is useful for enhancing this effect, as in the Murano glass handkerchief vase, and so are elegant trimmings like the bead trim shown here. A delicate lace decorates the baby pillows for the bed, while the bed linens, by the Monogrammed Linen Shop, have a caramel satin cotton border.

OVERLEAF Tiny rooms demand small but eloquent furniture. The macassar desk (as well as the matching chest at the foot of the bed) are in 1930s mode and are by Lucien Rollin, who specialises in recreating pieces from this era. The purple Liszt dressing table stool, which is from my range, is also inspired by 1930s designs.

The master bedroom is opposite the bathroom but I wanted to give my clients a sense of privacy, so you get into this area through a little lobby. At the end there is the second bedroom, which is now the study and dressing room – so this whole area is now a bedroom suite. On the walls in the bedroom I used a neutral linen fabric and the curtains are a horizontal-striped silk. The cupboards, which I put in and which extend all the way along the wall, are painted to look exactly like the linen-covered walls so that they disappear. Typical of my client, every drawer and every cupboard is organised so everything fits in. The client already had the painting. I threw in the purple velvet for the Liszt stool at the small desk and found a Murano handkerchief vase in purple and white. Because the flat is so tiny, everything had to be thought out like miniature magic.

The original second bedroom, which is now the study and dressing room, had to be and do all things for my client. Absolutely everything is built in and it really does work. Actually, I think it's like a 1930s boat. I built in the desk under the window, and there is a hanging cupboard which is only 40–50cm (16–20in) deep. It is done in veneer and bronze so it feels like the rest of the flat.

I think my clients have absolutely everything they want here. They can go back to their life in America or can go off travelling, and can shut the door on their pied-à-terre knowing that when they come back it will still be perfect. They love it because it's effortless and there's never going to be anything out of place. In a sense it's still a work in progress, but if my client buys something new for it, something old will have to go because there really isn't any more room.

OPPOSITE The cupboard in the study/dressing room was all minutely engineered and contains drawers for all my client's clothes, together with top cupboards and bookshelves, and a 120cm- (4ft-) wide bed drops down from it. It was really thought out, with a painting, a light and a shelf fixed in the cupboard space. It's incredibly comfortable and it works. I covered the shutters in this room in leather so that there was no fuss at the windows; he can open the shutters if he wants to, but it's not the greatest view.

OVERLEAF The cleverly engineered bed appears with its own clock, reading light, even its own photograph, and then it all folds up out of the way. It really is the answer for a small room.

# a hotel of home comforts

The charming Draycott Hotel, owned by the South African hotelier Adrian Gardner, occupies a terrace of three rather nice adjacent townhouses, now joined together but built in the 1890s in the Sir Hans Sloane style of architecture. I have been asked to titivate it gradually, as they don't want to close the hotel during the refurbishment. A great many literary and artistic figures have stayed here over the years, and still do today. What everybody loves about the Draycott is that it's a comfy hotel tucked away behind London's Sloane Square in what appears to be a private house. It is, in fact, a little jewel.

For the drawing room, which overlooks the hotel's lovely garden, I was asked to look at the collections of pictures, books, pots and goodness knows what that had been put together over the years, and make it seem more like someone's private room while at the same time reintegrating the art. The first thing I did was to mahoganise the fireplace which had previously been painted white and looked dreary. I then put down a neutral-coloured carpet which had a border around it, to delineate the space and give it a little bit of grandeur.

Next I added a pair of comfortable sofas flanking the fireplace. There had previously been sofas on either side of the fireplace, but if a couple came into the room, one of them would sit on each sofa, which messed up the seating for anybody else. I therefore pushed the sofas further back, which made space for two coffee tables between them. I also added a fender stool at the fireplace end of each of these sofas and an armchair at the other end of each, creating two groups around the fireplace.

OPPOSITE The main sitting room of the hotel opens on to a splendid garden. The paintings already belonged to the owners. The gilded brackets have interesting Chinese pots on them.

OVERLEAF The cushion is covered in my Hollybrook printed linen, and the sofa is upholstered in my Broughton Weave bird's-eye wool, which is brass-nailed to the frame. The rug was specially woven to my design, bringing in all the colours of the room. A fender covered in antique green leather provides extra seating.

BELOW AND OPPOSITE The comfortable small sofa covered in my Broughton Weave wool was used to create a fourth seating area. I think the Hollybrook linen chair and cushion, along with the lamp which we found somewhere in the hotel, create a bright touch that makes a potentially dark corner look cheerful. The aim was to make the room look as if nothing had really changed.

At the back of the room, I repositioned the drinks cupboard in order to put in a corner sofa. There are also some wandering chairs which can easily be pulled up. On the other side of the room there's another sofa, covered in a luxurious wool fabric. By reducing the size of the coffee table in front it, I was able to squeeze in two French chairs to make a group of four in a relatively small space. Now there are four good seating areas, which is enough for a hotel of this size.

I decided to paint the drawing room walls in a neutral shade in order to create a sympathetic background for the good paintings owned by the hotel, and then pump in some colour with the textiles. On some of the chairs and cushions, I used a floral linen from my own range to bring all the colours together. The curtains are in a green, red and buff stripe to echo the colours in the room. They are tied back to give a good view of the wonderful gardens, and at night the red taffeta under-curtain can be drawn to make the room cosy. The new chandelier is made to look as though it has been there for ever.

OPPOSITE Still in the same drawing room, a useful corner sofa is covered with my Campbell Damask in red ombre. The paintings from the hotel's private collection are lit with picture lights, and the addition of the brass arm lights at either end of the sofa makes a cosy corner in which to read. The useful table placed at the end of the sofa is the Mickey side table from my furniture collection, and the bronze bamboo Pagoda coffee table is also one of mine.

There was originally a bedroom suite downstairs, which had a little courtyard, and I was asked to turn the suite into a breakfast room. The room seemed rather dark and uninviting, and was reached by a rabbit warren of passages and doors. The first thing to do was to remove a door and include the passage into the decorative scheme of the new breakfast room. This we did by painting it an aqua blue to lighten it and turn the small bathroom into a comfortably sized cloakroom for the breakfast guests.

I also chose a palate of aqua and taupe for the new room and had a striéed carpet woven for the entire floor, in place of the previous rather busy one. The room needs to be able to turn into a private dining room too, so the banquette around the room can double as a pre-dinner sitting area. There is a fireplace in the room, and large windows overlooking a white painted courtyard area. In order to brighten the room, I had the alcoves either side of the fireplace mirrored, and hung brass leaf sconces on the mirror. These alcoves also have comfortable banquettes which work well as tables for two. The hotel had masses of their own chairs, so I re-stained them a darker shade and covered them in my Fursdon Weave.

OPPOSITE The breakfast room, formerly a bedroom, has a wraparound banquette covered in a figured stripe called Paracas, which echoes the plain stripe of my Canto Stripe wallpaper. On the walls are Hubbard floral paintings bought from Natural Curiosities — the enlarged size creates a sense of height.

OPPOSITE AND BELOW The brass leaf lights that are set on to the mirrored walls either side of the fireplace are by Vaughan. I re-covered an existing hotel chair in my Fursdon Weave to pick up the tones in the Paracas-covered banquette. The Paracas fabric combines the aquas and taupes, and adds a flash of gold. The tables all have mixed garden flowers, including hyacinths when available.

I was also asked to refurbish a suite of rooms, called the C.S. Lewis Suite, built into the eaves at the top of the hotel. It has a wonderful high ceiling, but the problem was that you walked into the middle of the room, opposite the window, which meant that there was nowhere very satisfactory for the bed. I therefore reconfigured the layout. Now you enter the suite, with the bathroom on your right and a walk-through lobby/dressing area on your left, into the room well to the left-hand side of the bed, which is now opposite the window. This also leaves enough space for a sofa, desk and bookcase.

A fabulous Gothic Revival chandelier was already in the room, so to complement it I created a half-tester bed using a delicate fabric. The main fabric of the suite, used for the curtains at the windows and the cushions on the bed, is another one of mine: Fairfield, a polished cotton print of loosely drawn lupins in blues and taupe, which provides the colour palette for the room.

Amongst all the pictures belonging to the hotel, we found some nice groups of prints that we could hang. What proved particularly exciting about this hotel was that they had some rather good things tucked away in store, which we have been able to restore and incorporate in the new look.

OPPOSITE In the C.S. Lewis Suite (named after the author because he often stayed at the Draycott) the Gothic Revival chandelier is very dominant. It was already in the room, as were a lot of the books for which the hotel is justly renowned. We used as much as possible of the existing furniture, but I made the half-tester on the bed using my Woodsford Sheer devoré. The colour scheme was kept to soft blues and taupe.

OVERLEAF A lovely mezzotint that we found elsewhere in the hotel looks handsome over the sofa. The blue and taupe theme even extends to some of the dust jackets on the books.

OPPOSITE AND BELOW All the rooms are named after famous literary characters who have stayed at the hotel. This suite is the C.S. Lewis Suite, and the visitors' book is on the desk, awaiting guests' comments. The framed photograph on the desk is of C.S. Lewis. The handsome desk looks antique but was actually made specially in order to house today's electrical requirements unobtrusively.

ABOVE The C.S. Lewis Suite can be booked with another charming room on the same floor. In this room we re-used the blue and brown paisley fabric that was still in good order. Originally there was a corona above the bed but we took it down and used the fabric to make matching blinds for the bedroom. We painted the walls this lovely pale blue, replacing the pale cream it had been, and this change immediately modernised the room. We also reframed and rehung the flower prints that we found in the hotel.

OPPOSITE We created a dressing room cum lobby entrance to the C.S. Lewis Suite — it had been a kitchen previously, but I think a proper entrance to a suite is important. The wallpaper is Bicton, a block stripe with metallic bands. The framed prints were found around the hotel and regrouped in this small space.

# the house of two cultures

My Chinese client, for whom I had already done two houses, rang me from Hong Kong one day and asked me a simple question: 'Are you busy?' He'd asked me that three times before and on each occasion I'd said, 'Of course not, I've got nothing to do whatsoever'. This time, as I suspected, he wanted me to go to China that week to see him, which I did.

He told me he had a house that he was pulling down because it was so ugly. My Scottish blood made me say, 'Don't pull it down, I'm sure we can do something with it'. He said, 'It's already gone' and, indeed, when I got there a large pile of rubble was all that was left of an old family house. Lots of bamboo scaffolding was going up on a massive site, set within a beautiful garden and park, mainly planted with magnolias and plum trees. In the distance, the land fell away to a distant lake.

As far as this client, is concerned, I know exactly how he wants to live, even given that it's a different life in China than it had been when he lived in England. He trusts me implicitly to deliver a really comfortable house and his wife knows that she is also going to get what she wants.

The floor plan had already been done before I got there. The considerations in terms of space were that my client is an important figure in China, and therefore a certain amount of 'ambassadorial' entertaining was going to be taking place, which explains why the drawing room in particular is so massive.

The entrance hall is very like one in an 18th-century English house. When you drive up, you come to an enormous door under a huge double-height porch. The weather in China is quite extreme – freezing cold in the winter; hot, heavy and humid in the summer. It can also rain very heavily in spring and autumn, so a substantial entrance is very useful.

OPPOSITE The staircase hall shows this house's mixture of Orient and Occident in both architecture and objects.

RIGHT AND BELOW On the spinach-green lacquer of the staircase I hung a collection of drawings of grand English buildings from Vitruvius Britannicus, first published in the early 18th century. I designed the bronze staircase in an Oriental pattern and it was made in China. The lantern was made to echo the early 19th-century English wall lights I found.

The main entrance leads into a very large hall which is dominated by an incredible picture of Buddha, facing you. It is very old and special, making it impossible to have any other pictures in the hall. I decided to contrast the picture with over-scaled carved Chinese Chippendale consoles and looking glasses and with Chinese pots on the consoles. This was the first of many instances where I deliberately mixed the two very different cultures in one house. My client is obsessed with English life, so although I was perfectly happy to give him a particularly English house in Sussex, I felt that as we were in China we should include Chinese detail.

That's why I decided that every cornice and every air-conditioning vent should be Chinese fretwork, every arch should have a Chinese feel, and that the ironwork on the staircase should be Chinese ironwork. I also thought it important to do as much as possible of that work in China itself. With the windows overlooking the gardens, for instance, I wanted to have dark wood fretwork screens so that one wouldn't feel so exposed to the garden; the screens make you look through them to glimpse something wonderful on the other side. Referencing classical Chinese screens, they were made in China. Although we were working with the Hong Kong-based architects on the major building, I commissioned Ron Lambell of Jones Lambell to help us with the interior architecture. This meant sending a young architect to live on site for about six months! Together we designed the interior architectural details.

Either side of the entrance hall you see the garden, then you go down long corridors to the entertaining rooms on the other side of the house, facing the lake. The entire house has stone floors and stone-coloured walls along the corridors, punctuated with black wood covings and arches. In the side hall there's a grand English-style staircase with wrought iron balustrades and dominated by a very large lantern. I wanted to dissociate the stairway from all of that and make it separate, so I painted it in a spinach-green lacquer with a stair runner in green and bronze with scrolls in a gold colour. Pursuing my cultural-mix idea, I decided that this was where I was going to hang black and white pictures of rather grand English facades.

OPPOSITE A view of the internal gardens through the Chinese fretwork screens. The beaten silver bowl came from Altfield in Hong Kong and holds one of the few plants I managed to buy in the Chinese flower market.

All the public rooms are very large but the drawing room is massive – big enough to have substantial seating areas at both ends, plus another seating arrangement in the middle. At the four corners of the room are archways with mirrored arches. Beneath one of these at each end, facing each other, is a mahogany door, and beneath the other pair of facing archways, which are mirrored, we put consoles with oval mirrors above them and big flower arrangements. Large cranberry glass trumpet vases are filled with beautiful silk flowers, arranged by John Carter to look as real as possible. The local flower market is not yet of Covent Garden standard, so buying fresh flowers is a problem.

Defining the areas of the room in this way made the space easier to deal with. The sitting areas at the ends of the room each have a big sofa, which fits within the pair of pilasters. With each sofa are two armchairs, a couple of bergères and a big coffee table, so six to eight people can be seated comfortably at each end of the room.

In the middle of the room, we placed a Victorian 'sociable', with drum tables and little chairs to draw up. In front of the windows, we put another French settee with tables and lamps either side and a couple of chairs, and on the other side we placed another marble inlay table with more chairs. And there's still plenty of space to stand and talk and to gather for big parties.

I commissioned a huge rug in France, copied from something I found in a 1930s magazine, and we had it woven in all the favourite Chinese colours – soft creams, gold, touches of red. I've learned over the years that the Chinese really love red, and I've also discovered that there's nothing better than some red thrown into a room because it warms the room immediately. I used a teal blue colour as well, and some yellow. It's all there in the rugs and in the bergères which echo the rugs.

OPPOSITE I commissioned this sculpture of a plum blossom branch from the renowned sculptress Lin Sproule. The delicate gold blossoms are set on to the bronze branch. The sculpture features small insects, including a cricket, and there is a spider on the rose quartz base. When the Buddhist priest came to bless the house, he was particularly taken by this piece.

OPPOSITE This is one end of the very large drawing room where we had to provide seating for well over 20 people. I had the carpet made specially for this room to my own design, taking inspiration from 1930s Chinese-inspired rugs. The beautiful brush painting is from my client's collection.

OVERLEAF The opposite end of the drawing room is dominated by another superlative painting, which is hung on a background of my Sonora damask in beige overprinted in gold for a shimmer. The cushions, too, have a sheen.

BELOW The sconces are French and echo the dramatic central chandelier.

RIGHT In the dining room I specified a faded Roman pink, plaster-effect panelling, and mirrors were inset into this – I needed the mirrors because I wanted to set some girandoles I had found on to them. We put them on to faceted mirror back plates for even more glitter. The effect is echoed by the mirrored back to the sideboard, one of a pair made for the room. The round table seating 22 was made for the room by David Linley. The chairs, which are reproductions of 18th-century French chairs, are covered in chrysanthemum-motif fabric by Rubelli. I had the carpet made by Braquenié following references of antique Chinese rugs.

The drawing room is the showiest room of the house so the cushions are all satins and silks, picking up the colours of the rugs and of the paintings that I hung above the two sofas at the ends of the room. I had felt that they needed to be large landscapes, and so on one of my visits to this remote house, I was taken to a marvellous hangar to look at my client's collection of traditional brush paintings. Endless pictures were unrolled for my inspection, and what was lucky was that I found two that were perfect. My favourite, I think, is the Harvest Moon (shown on page 211). Chinese paintings are often rolled and then kept in their rolls and boxes for quite a long time – it is quite unusual to have them shown. I therefore felt it was important for these to have only simple water-gilt frames. Black frames would not have been right in this room.

The dining room was a huge square space. We were responsible for the interior architecture, so decided to panel this room. We had to contend with some columns which support the corridor that goes round the house, so having got stuck with these columns, I decided to make a virtue of necessity and turn it all into an 'architectural conversation'. Inset in some of the panels we placed mirrors on which we hung other mirrors and wall lights, which gives a very glamorous effect at night. A wonderful chandelier hangs over the table. The wall sconces are English but were too small for the scale of the room, so I mounted them on mirrors with thumb cuts, because I wanted to make them more important.

The dining table had to seat 22 and as the Chinese like to sit at a round table, the room had to accommodate it. David Linley made this vast round table on a huge base, which had to come in four parts to be fitted together. When the table arrived, it was so enormous that the only way to clean it was to put rubber bags on your knees and then get on all fours in the middle of the table! The wood is mahogany, with black Chinese fretwork inlaid around the edge, so, like the room, it is both occidental and oriental.

OPPOSITE Silver adds to the glitter in the dining room – I bought the charming turn-of-the-century oil and vinegar barrels. Two silver plate wine coolers make very good pots for the orchid plants.

OPPOSITE AND BELOW In the breakfast room I asked Mark Done to paint the walls with a Chinese scene picking up the shapes of the trees that can be seen outside the windows. I was very excited to find the chandelier, which is verdigris bronze oak leaves. As the room was not symmetrical, we used three wall lights, one large and two slightly smaller, that I commissioned specially to go with the chandelier. These lights appear to grow out of the painted trees, which is great fun.

At the beginning of this job, I had no idea what artwork I was going to be given, if any, so I had to decorate each room with enough detail for it to survive without any artwork. But when decorating the dining room I was fortunate to discover that we had four panels that are very important poems, and two landscape pictures for the middle. For the rest of the room I had wanted to use richer colours, but it wasn't the place for a red, English-style dining room, so I worked with black, a beautiful coral shade and creams. I saw a 1920s rug with a black Chinese border – there was no question of buying an antique carpet in these sizes – and so we had a carpet made, copying various elements from the 1920s rug, and making up the middle.

On the other side of the house is the TV room, again with huge windows overlooking the lake and garden. I put gold and yellow fabric on the wall above the dado rail. The English-style fireplace was made in China, and a modern chest is combined with one of my client's wonderful Chinese paintings. On top of one side of the chest are jade ornaments, and on the other side a collection of ivory fruits and vegetables that I found and had mounted on blocks. There's a fantastic jade object – my client is a great collector of jade – on top of the fireplace. There's also a double, back-to-back, massive, old-fashioned Howard sofa in the middle of the room. On one half you can just sit by the fire, and on the other side you've got the biggest television ever known to man.

OPPOSITE A corner of the mahjong room, richly wallpapered in a gold flower which echoes the painting of a tulip by Sophie Coryndon. There is a red-and-gold theme in this room, quite deliberately, as it is very auspicious to the Chinese – and, of course, the mahjong room had to have such a scheme.

RIGHT This is the television room, which has two sofas, back to back, one facing the television and the other the fireplace, which, like many in the house, I had made to a European design. The dominant theme here is the Imperial yellow ribbed cotton on the walls, set off by the French embroidered tapestry cushions. The carpet was made by Parsua.

BELOW The TV-facing sofa, with a supremely comfortable Howard chair and run-up covered in a dark green strié velvet.

LEFT In his English home I'd given my client a proper wood-panelled library, and he wanted the same thing here, so we had great fun with this. First I bought a fireplace in a handsome marble, and on either side I put carved wood and gilded mirrors above rather beautiful serpentine chests. My client is very keen on birds and animals so I bought him some interesting books for the library, and he also filled it with his own Chinese books. We had a great big partner's desk made in the English style, and threw in a couple of Chinese Chippendale chairs and a wooden architect's staircase that echoes the staircase we put into the house.

BELOW Chinese books are stored in a bookcase carved in a Chinese design.

OPPOSITE AND BELOW The billiard room walls are covered in red carriage cloth and the curtains are in the same fabric. The Chopin bench, which is from my own range, is covered in my red and purple Voluta Stripe velvet. On the floor is a contemporary Tai Ping carpet made in China to our own colourway.

Sweeping up the house's staircase to the first floor, you go down the central corridor to the master bedroom suite – another room with fabulous views over the lake. In the bedroom is a half-tester bed, plus there is a sofa in front of the television. On the walls is my Belzoro Filigrane linen in pale blue, overprinted in a silver fretwork design – this brings a shimmer to the walls. The fabric of the curtains is a floral printed silk called Pemberley from my range. The flowers have a hand-painted feel and are reminiscent of early Chinese flower paintings. The stool at the end of the bed is covered in a charming brocade from Claremont.

While I was decorating this house down to the last details of the two cultures, I had the idea of commissioning a sculpture from Lin Sproule, whose work I had spotted in *World of Interiors*. The owner of the house has a plum garden; such gardens are really special in China and are thought to be very lucky, so I decided to do a branch of plum blossom for him (shown on page 209). This involved going to see Peter Adler, who deals in rocks and crystals, where I bought a piece of rose quartz. The florist John Carter found a branch of flowering plum blossom, and Lin Sproule went back on the train to Cornwall with the branch, which she then cast in bronze. From that bronze branch she had the blossoms coming out in gold, with all the lucky Chinese creatures, like butterflies and crickets. The client was over the moon and, mercifully, so was the Buddhist priest who came to bless the house. They'd never seen anything like it.

Perhaps the most extraordinary thing about this unique house, with its cultural mix of Chinese and English taste, is that it has been designed so that my client, who for health reasons has to take exercise (which he hates to do), can walk all the way around it on a sort of track without going outdoors. I suppose if you think about it, it could almost be described as an *enfilade à la chinoise*!

OPPOSITE In the master bedroom, which is very European in inspiration, the Tai Ping carpet is unbelievably luxurious. The rice paper botanicals are exquisite – they were part of a book I came across in the client's store and I had them framed in a simple water gilt frame to make the most of their fragility.

RIGHT The walls of the guest bedroom are covered in Lomasi, a bold design comprised of vertical lines of lilac, which is part of my range. Over the bed are mirror-framed botanical prints of lilac. The French cane bedhead is trellised in the same pale blue as the walls, and the bed linen echoes the trellis pattern. Flanking the bed is a pair of Italian bedside tables.

OPPOSITE The very English-style cupboard opposite the bed hides the television and also houses extra bed linen – all the guest bedrooms have good closets in their dressing areas. This bedroom, like the others, shows a good mixture of English comfort and Occidental details. The armchair and stool are covered in Lomasi fabric to match the walls.

BELOW LEFT We anchored the bedroom with black wood Chinese furniture, as in this side table.

BELOW RIGHT The air-conditioning grilles were made in a Chinese fretwork design and set within the cornicing.

ABOVE We decided to give this bathroom a glamorously 1930s feel, with the panelled mosaic for the walls and the mother-of-pearl dressing table made by Garrison Rousseau. I had great fun buying the beautiful dressing-table set bottles and the Bakelite tray. The stool, my Liszt, is covered in blue Maroquin from Manuel Canovas.

OPPOSITE We softened the rather hard windows in this bathroom with a sliding fretwork screen. The Lalique bowl light on the ceiling came from Carlton Davidson. The mirrored doors lead to a separate shower and loo.

# index

Figures in *italics* refer to pages with
photographs.

# *author's acknowledgements*

It would not have been possible to create any of these houses or this book without a great many wonderful people.

I am immensely grateful to all my clients who have so generously allowed me to photograph their homes.

A very special thank you goes to Simon Brown who took all the photographs for this book, with the exception of the house in China. He made the whole process great fun, and delivered a beautiful product. Thank you also to John Butlin who did an equally great job for me in China. It was my lucky day when Meredith Etherington-Smith agreed to write the book with me, and she made the entire process seem easy.

I am very lucky to have a hardworking and diligent design team, led brilliantly by Georg Lauth. We often have to spend long times away from home together and they have always been enthusiastic and good humoured. My complicated life and everchanging travel plans have been calmly dealt with by Buffy Fitzgerald, and the very difficult task of being my children and working for the company has been brilliantly handled by both my son Max Konig and my daughter Alice Sharples. I am lucky also to,have a supportive team in every angle of my business and a huge thank you goes to them all, past and present.

I have worked on some of these projects with teams of architects, and I would particularly like to thank Ron Lambell, who worked with me in China, and Pietro Brunetti, who spent months there watching the works take shape. In New York we worked with Kevin Lichten and Maritta Alfonso, and Douglas Reetz, which made working across the pond a whole lot easier. The precision and workmanship delivered by Chaletbau Matti and Cornelia Beyer in Switzerland was a joy.

John Carter is the genius behind all the flowers in my life and he has done many of the houses in this book. I was lucky to find a kindred spirit in Donnie Nightshade when I needed flowers in New York.

Len Carter, the Garveys and Henry van der Vijver and their teams certainly made life in China a lot more lively.

Of course I have worked also with the most amazing craftsmen, art dealers, antique dealers and so on to achieve many of these interiors, and a massive thank you goes to them all.

Last but by no means least, thank you to Cindy Richards, Gillian Haslam and Sally Powell and all the team from Cico Books for being so patient and hardworking to produce this book.

ABOVE I first saw Kate Malone's work at a joint exhibition in London of Adrian Sassoon and Robilant & Voena. This overscaled crystaline glazed stoneware pine cone completely blew me away and I called my client in New York. Luckily he felt the same way, and this piece now occupies pride of place on a William IV marble-topped table in the hall.